CANON EOS R6 II POCKET GUIDE

TABLE OF CONTENTS

01 PRE-SHOOT CHECKLIST

Check these settings before you head out with your camera!

SETTING	MY PREFERRED SETTING
☑ Shooting Mode	....
☑ White Balance Setting	....
☑ ISO Setting	....
☑ Exposure Compensation	....
☑ Focus Mode	....
☑ Focus Method	....
☑ Drive Mode	....
☑ Metering Mode	....
☑ Picture Style	....
☑ Bracketing Setting	....
☑ Highlight Alert Setting	....
☑ File Format: RAW, JPEG, or RAW & JPEG	....
☑ Battery Fully Charged and In Camera	....
☑ Memory Card(s) Formatted and In Camera	....

02 BUTTONS, DIALS, AND SCREENS

CAMERA BODY TOP

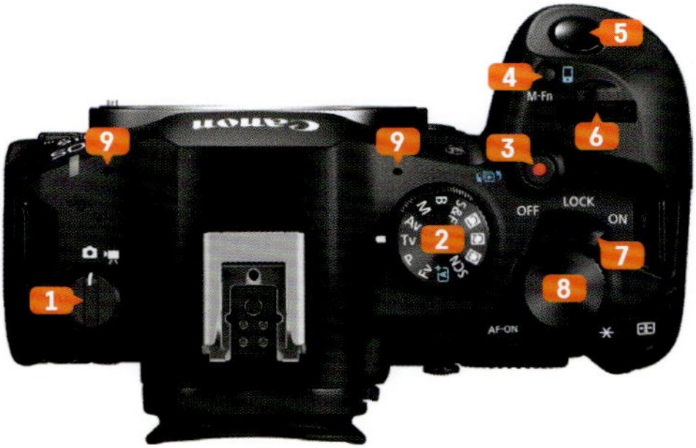

1. **Photo/Video Switch:** Switch between still photos and movie mode.
2. **Mode Dial:** Turn to select the shooting mode.
3. **Movie Shooting Button/Movie-Photo Playback Toggle:** Press to start/stop recording a movie/Use to toggle between movies and photos during playback.
4. **Multi-Function (M-Fn) Button/Send to Smartphone Button:** Press this button in combination with turning the Main dial to set ISO, drive mode, AF (autofocus) operation, white balance, and flash exposure compensation/Use to send images to a smartphone.
5. **Shutter Button:** Press halfway to activate autofocus; press all the way to take a photo.

6. **Main Dial:** Use this dial to set the shutter speed, aperture, and other settings.
7. **Power Switch/Multi-Function Lock Switch:** Turns the camera on and off. Lock function prevents settings from being changed if you accidentally operate the Main dial, Quick Control dials, Multi-controller, touch-screen panel, or the lens's control ring.
8. **Quick Control Dial 2:** Use this dial to set exposure compensation and aperture while in Manual shooting mode, etc.
9. **Microphones:** Records audio when recording movies.

CAMERA BODY BACK

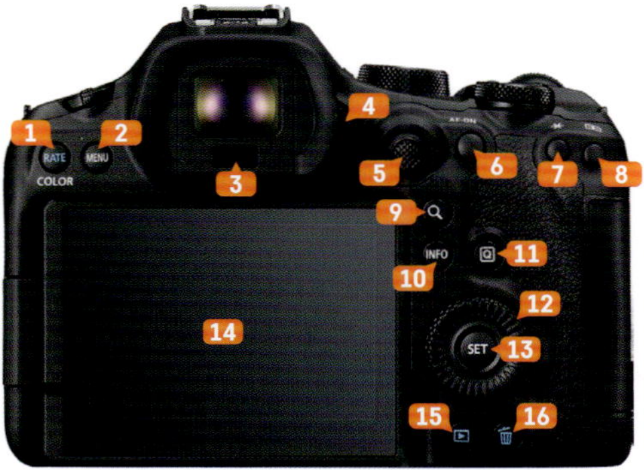

1. **COLOR/RATE Button:** Used to set the color mode/Apply star ratings to images during playback.
2. **MENU Button:** Press to bring up menu options.
3. **Viewfinder Sensor:** Senses when you're looking through the viewfinder and activates the viewfinder display.

4. **Dioptric Adjustment Knob:** Turn left or right to make the viewfinder display sharp.

5. **Multi-Controller:** Use for operations such as white balance correction, autofocus (AF) point movement, magnifying the frame during playback, Quick Control setting adjustments, etc. Can also select or set menu items.

6. **AF Start (AF-ON) Button:** Press to engage the autofocus.

7. **AE Lock Button:** Use to lock exposure.

8. **AF Point Selection Button:** Use to select the desired AF-point.

9. **Magnify/Reduce Button:** Use to adjust image playback options (index view, zoom in, and zoom out).

10. **INFO Button:** Press to cycle through views displaying different information.

11. **Quick Control (Q) Button:** Use to access the Quick Control screen.

12. **Quick Control Dial 1:** Use to navigate menus, move focus points, etc.

13. **SET Button:** Use to finalize a setting and return to a previous screen.

14. **Screen:** Displays multiple features, options, and settings for shooting and playback.

15. **Playback Button:** Press to view the last image taken.

16. **Erase Button:** Use to erase the current photo on display.

CAMERA BODY FRONT

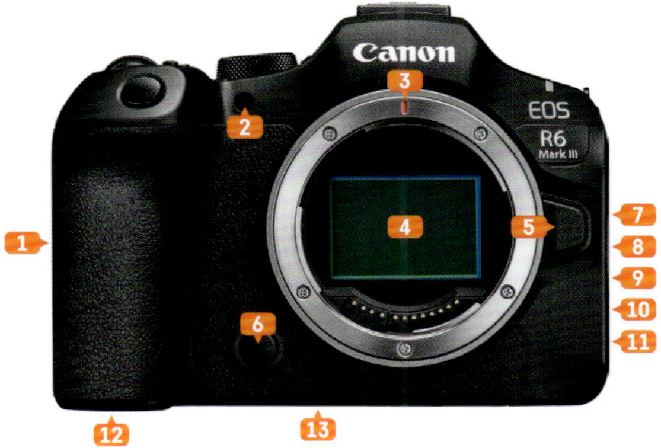

1. **Dual Memory Card Slots (Under Cover, Side):** Supports SD/SDHC/SDXC memory cards.
2. **AF-Assist Beam/Self-Timer:** Lights up area in front of camera in low light/Blinks when Self-Timer is active.
3. **Lens Mounting Mark:** Used to line up lens and camera when mounting a lens.
4. **Image Sensor:** The 32.5-megapixel full-frame CMOS sensor.
5. **Lens Release Button:** Press to remove the lens.
6. **Depth-of-Field Preview Button:** Press to see the current depth of field.
7. **Microphone Terminal:** The port to connect an external microphone to the camera.
8. **Digital Terminal:** The port to connect to digital devices.
9. **Headphones:** The port to connect headphones to camera.
10. **HDMI Out Terminal:** The port to connect an HDMI mini cable.

11. Remote Control Terminal: The port to connect a remote control to the camera.

12. Battery and Battery Compartment Cover (Bottom of Camera): Open to access the battery compartment.

13. Tripod Socket (Bottom of Camera): A standard socket for a tripod or monopod.

SHOOTING SCREEN (STILL PHOTO)

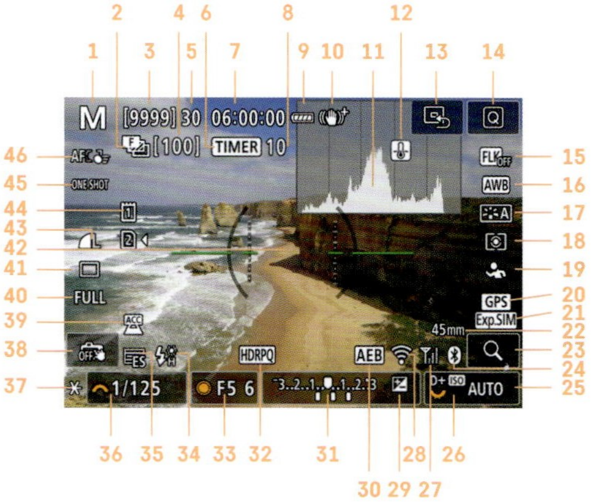

Each time you press the INFO button, the information display will change. The display will show only the settings currently applied.

Note: Viewfinder display positions will vary for some items.

1. **Shooting Mode**
2. **Focus Bracketing/HDR Mode/Multiple Exposure Shooting/ Pre-Continuous Shooting**
3. **Number of Available Shots/Sec. Until Self-Timer Shoots**
4. **Number of Remaining Shots for Focus Bracketing/Multiple Exposure Shots**
5. **Maximum Burst/Number of Remaining Multiple Exposure Shots**
6. **Interval Timer Shooting/Bulb Timer Shooting**
7. **Movie Recording Time Available**
8. **Number of Remaining Interval Timer Shots**
9. **Battery Level**
10. **Image Stabilizer (IS Mode)**
11. **Histogram**
12. **Overheat Warning/Still Photo Image Quality Warning**
13. **Set AF Point to Center**
14. **Quick Control Button**
15. **Anti-Flicker Shooting**
16. **White Balance/White Balance Correction**
17. **Picture Style**
18. **Metering Mode**
19. **Subject to Detect**
20. **GPS**
21. **Display Simulation/OVF Simulation View Assist**
22. **Focal Length**
23. **Magnify Button**
24. **Bluetooth Function**
25. **ISO Speed**
26. **Highlight Tone Priority**

27. Wi-Fi Signal Strength/Airplane Mode
28. Wi-Fi Function
29. Exposure Compensation
30. AEB/FEB (Auto Exposure Bracketing/Flash Exposure Bracketing)
31. Exposure Level Indicator (Exposure Compensation Amount/ AEB Range)
32. HDRPQ
33. Aperture Value
34. Flash Ready/FE Lock/High-Speed Sync
35. Electronic Shutter/Silent Shutter
36. Shutter Speed
37. AE Lock (Exposure Lock)
38. Touch Shutter/Create Folder
39. Accessory Attached Indicator
40. Still Photo Cropping/Aspect Ratio
41. Drive Mode
42. AF Point (1-Point AF)
43. Image Quality
44. Card
45. AF Operation
46. AF Area

SHOOTING SCREEN (MOVIE)

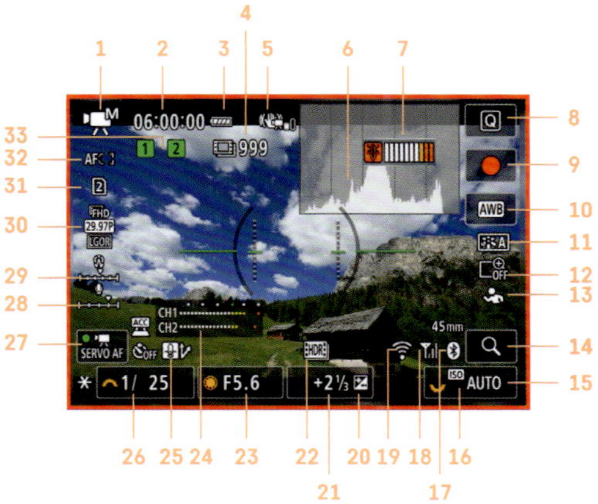

Each time you press the INFO button, the information display will change. The display will show only the settings currently applied. The screen will change depending on if you are in standby mode or a movie recording is in progress.

Note: Viewfinder display positions will vary for some items.

1. **Movie Shooting Mode**
2. **Movie Recording Time Available**
3. **Battery Level**
4. **Number of Movies that Can Be Recorded**
5. **Image Stabilizer**

6. Histogram (Brightness/RGB)
7. Overheating Warning
8. Quick Control Button
9. Movie Shooting Button (Start Recording)
10. White Balance/White Balance Correction
11. Picture Style
12. Digital Zoom
13. Subject to Detect
14. Magnify Button
15. ISO Speed
16. Highlight Tone Priority
17. Bluetooth Function
18. Wi-Fi Signal Strength
19. Wi-Fi Function
20. Exposure Compensation
21. Exposure Level Indicator (Metering Levels)
22. HDR Movie Recording
23. Aperture Value
24. Audio Recording Level Indicator
25. Overheat Control
26. Shutter Speed
27. Movie Servo AF
28. Audio Recording Level (Manual/Line Input)
29. Headphone Volume
30. Movie Recording Size
31. Card Used for Recording and Playback
32. AF Area
33. Recording Status (Left: Main Movie; Right: Proxy/Sub Movie)

03 ESSENTIAL MODES AND SETTINGS

SHOOTING MODES

Rotate the Mode dial to select the desired shooting mode.

Fv (Flexible-Priority AE):

Photo: Shutter speed, aperture, and ISO are all set automatically, then you can change one, two, or all three settings to get your desired look (shallow depth of field or slow shutter speed, for example). The settings you don't change will automatically be adjusted by the camera using the current metering mode.

Movie: Auto exposure mode, where the cameras sets everything.

P (Program AE):

Photo: The camera sets the shutter speed and aperture based on metering info and current ISO.

Movie: Auto exposure mode, where the cameras sets everything.

Tv (Time Value or Shutter Speed Priority):

Photo: You set the shutter speed, and the camera sets the aperture based on metering info and current ISO.

Movie: Set the shutter speed for movie recording. It is limited by the current frames per second setting.

Av (Aperture Value or Aperture Priority):

Photo: You set the aperture and the camera sets the shutter speed based on metering info and current ISO. Range of available apertures depends on the attached lens.

Movie: You set the aperture and the camera sets the shutter speed.

M (Manual):

Photo: You set ISO, shutter speed, and aperture. Refer to the exposure level indicator.

Movie: You set ISO, shutter speed, and aperture. The available shutter speeds vary by the set frame rate.

Bulb:

Photo: Used for long exposures, the shutter stays open as long as you hold down the shutter button. Use the Main dial to set the aperture.

Movie: Auto exposure mode where the cameras sets everything.

S&F (Slow/Fast):

Photo: Same as P (Program AE).

Movie: (See Chapter 4.)

C1, C2, C3 (Custom Shooting Modes):

Photo: Use the setup menu to set a custom shooting mode.

Movie: Use the setup menu to set a custom movie recording.

SCN (Special Scene Mode):

Photo: The camera settings are chosen depending on the scene type the photographer selects from the list.

Movie: There are four special scenes for movies, and the camera settings are adjusted depending on which is chosen.

A+ (Scene Intelligent Auto):

Photo: The camera assesses the scene and sets the optimum settings automatically. It will even adjust the focus on both still and moving subjects.

Movie: The camera detects the scene and automatically sets all settings.

METERING MODES

Press the Q button, then use the Multi-controller to navigate to and select the metering mode icon. Then use the Main dial or the Multi-controller to cycle through the metering modes. Press the SET button, or use the MENU > Photo Shooting (Exposure) > Metering mode.

Evaluative: General-purpose mode suited for most situations and subjects (photos and movies).

Partial: Uses 6.2% of the area at the center of the screen for determining exposure. Good choice when there is very bright light around the subject (photos only).

Spot: Uses 2.9% of the area at the center of the screen. Use when you need to meter a specific part of the scene.

Center-Weighted Average: The camera analyzes the whole scene to determine exposure, but places more emphasis on info at the center of the screen (photos only).

EXPOSURE COMPENSATION

Press the shutter button halfway down, then rotate the Quick Control Dial 1 to adjust exposure compensation, from –3 (darker) to +3 (lighter) stops, in 1/3-stop increments. To cancel the exposure compensation, set the value back to 0.

Note: The exposure compensation you set will remain in effect until you change it; it does not return to 0 when the camera is turned off.

FOCUS OPERATION

MENU > AF (Operation/Area) > AF Operation

1-Shot AF: Focus starts when the shutter button is pressed halfway, then locks when focus is achieved. Best for stationary subjects.

Servo: Focus starts when the shutter button is pressed halfway and continues to focus until photo is taken. Best for moving subjects.

AI Focus: Automatically switches between 1-Shot AF and Servo depending on what the subject is doing when the shutter button is pressed halfway down.

Movie Servo AF: Set the Photo/Movie Recording switch to Movie. When you open AF Operation you can select Movie Servo AF. This sets the camera to focus on the subject continuously when recording movies.

Note: For **Manual focus**, set the AF/MF switch on the lens to MF, and rotate the focus ring on the lens barrel to focus. For RF lenses that do not have a focus mode switch, navigate to MENU > AF (Screen 1) > AF Operations > Focus mode > MF.

AUTOFOCUS AREA

MENU > AF (AF Operation/Area) > AF Area

Spot AF: The camera focuses on the smallest possible area, even narrower than 1-Point AF.

1-Point AF: The camera focuses using a single point for critical focus.

Expand AF Area: The camera uses one AF point as well as the points adjacent and nearby to that focus point to help focus. Helpful for moving subjects that are difficult to track with 1-Point AF.

Expand AF Area: Around: The camera creates an even larger area around one AF point to find focus.

Flexible Zone AF 1: Default is set as square Zone AF frame.

Flexible Zone AF 2: Default is set as vertical rectangular Zone AF frame.

Flexible Zone AF 3: Default is set as horizontal rectangular Zone AF frame.

Whole Area AF: The camera decides what to focus on using the whole area.

ADDITIONAL AUTOFOCUS OPTIONS

Whole Area Tracking Servo AF: MENU > AF (AF operation/ area) > Whole area tracking servo AF. When the AF Operation is set to Servo you can turn Whole Area Tracking Servo to:

On: The AF area switches to Whole Area AF to track subjects across the entire screen while the shutter button is halfway pressed.

Off: The subjects are only tracked between the currently selected AF points when the shutter button is halfway pressed.

Move the AF Point or Zone AF Frame: Press the AF Point selection button, then use the Multi-controller to move the point to the desired location and press the Set button. To center the AF point, press the Multi-controller straight in. You can also tap directly on the screen to select the focus point.

Subject to Detect: MENU > AF (Subject detection) > Subject to Detect. Picks the type of subject to look for when using subject tracking. The choices are: Auto, People, Animals, Vehicles, and None.

Eye Detection: MENU > AF (Subject detection) > Eye Detection. Select Auto to have the camera pick the eye, or select Right Eye or Left Eye in the menu.

Manual Focus Peaking: MENU > AF (MF related) > MF Peaking Settings. When manually focusing, focus peaking informs you that focus has been achieved by lighting up the edges of the in-focus subject in the specified color. You can turn it on and set the sensitivity (Level) and the color.

DRIVE MODES

Press the M-Fn (Multi-Function) button and select the drive mode option, then rotate the Main dial to select the desired mode.

Single Shooting: The camera takes a single shot every time the shutter button is fully pressed.

High-Speed Continuous Shooting +: The camera takes up to 12 frames per second (mechanical shutter) and 40 frames per second (electronic shutter) when you press and hold the shutter button.

High-Speed Continuous Shooting: The camera takes up to 6.2 frames per second (mechanical shutter) and 20 frames per second (electronic shutter).

Low-Speed Continuous Shooting: The camera takes up to 3 frames per second (mechanical shutter) and 5 frames per second (electronic shutter) when you press and hold the shutter button.

Self-Timer 10: Sets the self-timer for 10 seconds.

Self-Timer 2: Sets the self-timer for 2 seconds.

Self-Timer C: Sets the self-timer to shoot continuously in 10 seconds for the number of frames specified (2–10) in the drive mode or on the Quick Control screen.

WHITE BALANCE

Press the M-Fn (Multi-Function) button, select the White Balance option, then rotate the Main dial to select the desired setting.

Auto [AWB] (Ambience priority) setting is the best for most situations.

Auto [AWBW] (White Priority) is best when you want to reduce a warm color cast.

White balance can be set to shift colors warmer, cooler, or keep them accurate. Other settings are all matched to different lighting types. For truest colors, pick the type of lighting being used to illuminate the scene.

IMAGE QUALITY

MENU > Photo Shooting (Image quality/size) > Image Quality.

Use the Main dial to select the RAW quality, and the Quick Control Dial 1 to select the JPEG/HEIF quality (Large, Medium, or Small). Press SET to set the Image Quality. Using the Quick menu, it is easy to see and adjust what file types are being saved to either of the memory cards.

RAW/C-RAW (Compact RAW): The RAW data from the image sensor is recorded each time a photo is taken. The C-RAW version is a compressed RAW file that takes up less space.

RAW+JPEG: If you have selected both a RAW and JPEG option, the camera saves two files each time the shutter button is pressed: a RAW file and a JPEG file. You also decide the size of the JPEG (Large, Medium, or Small).

JPEG: The camera saves a JPEG file each time the shutter button is pressed. You also decide the size of the JPEG.

HEIF: This file type is used for HDR shooting and can be converted to JPEG after shooting.

04 OTHER HELPFUL SETTINGS

DISPLAY SIMULATION

MENU > Photo Shooting (Assist Shooting 1) > Display Simulation. This feature displays a simulation of the current exposure and depth of field that more closely matches the actual brightness of your shots.

Exposure + DOF: The displayed image brightness will be close to the actual exposure and depth of field of the resulting image. Exposure compensation will change the simulated brightness of the image accordingly. Changes to the aperture will change the depth of field.

Exposure: The displayed image brightness will be close to the actual exposure of the resulting image. Exposure compensation will change the simulated brightness of the image.

Exposure Only During DOF: Shows the exposure simulation and depth of field only when you press the button that is assigned to Depth-of-Field Preview.

Disable: The image is displayed at the standard brightness at all times, regardless of exposure settings or exposure compensation.

PICTURE STYLES

MENU > Photo Shooting (Color/Tone/Dynamic Range) > Color Mode > Picture Styles

Allows you to adjust settings for JPEG images. Adjustable settings are **Sharpness (Strength, Fineness, Threshold), Contrast, Saturation, Color Tone, Filter Effect (Monochrome),** and **Toning Effect (Monochrome)**. Seven preset picture controls can all be adjusted: **A (Auto), S (Standard), P (Portrait), L (Landscape), FD (Fine Detail), N (Neutral), F (Faithful), M (Monochrome)**. The Monochrome picture control also has four color filters: Yellow, Orange, Red, Green. Finally, there are also three User-Defined Picture Styles, which allow you to customize any of the styles for easy access.

CUSTOM WHITE BALANCE

Setting a custom white balance can help you get the best color when you're shooting under mixed lighting:

1. Take a photo of a white card (or white wall) under the mixed lighting at the scene. Be sure to fill the screen (this may require you to switch to Manual focus to create the exposure).

2. Select MENU > Photo Shooting (White balance/Quality correction) > White Balance Settings > Custom White Balance.

3. The last photo taken will be shown (if not, select it with the Quick Control Dial 1). Press SET and select OK.

4. Select MENU > Photo Shooting (White balance/Quality correction) > White Balance Settings > White Balance, and select the Custom White Balance icon.

COLOR SPACE

MENU > Photo Shooting (Color/Tone/Dynamic Range) > Color Space

sRGB: Smaller color space. Best when images are used directly from camera.

Adobe RGB: Larger color space. Best used when images will be edited with post-processing software.

HIGHLIGHT ALERT (BLINKIES)

MENU > Playback (Various Settings) > Highlight Alert

Select Enable so that clipped highlights will blink, alerting you to possible overexposure when playing back images. To obtain more detail in those areas, adjust exposure settings or exposure compensation and shoot again.

NOISE REDUCTION

MENU > Shooting (White Balance/Quality Correction) > Long Exposure Noise Reduction

Reduces noise in images with shutter speeds of 1 second or longer. Doubles the time needed to save image to memory card. Choices are Auto, Enable, and Disable. Auto is usually the best choice.

MENU > Photo Shooting (Balance/Quality Correction) > High ISO Speed NR

Reduces noise in images taken at high ISO settings. Use Standard for default, Low for less noise reduction, and High for more noise reduction.

MENU > Movie Recording (Sound-rec. Settings) > Audio Settings > Built-in Microphone > Audio Noise Reduction

Works to reduce lens sounds when using the built in microphones. Can be set to Disable (no noise reduction), Enable (automatically applies noise reduction while recording), and High (applies more noise reduction than enable).

AUTO ISO

MENU > Photo Shooting (Exposure) > ISO Speed Settings

Within the ISO Speed Settings, you can select Auto for the ISO Speed, then use the Auto Range option to set the minimum and maximum ISO settings to define the range that the camera can use. You can also set the minimum shutter speed to ensure that the camera does not lower the shutter speed too much; this helps reduce camera shake and blurry images.

EXPOSURE BRACKETING

You can bracket a set of three exposures up to +/–3 stops in 1/3-stop increments:

1. Select MENU > Photo Shooting (Exposure) > Exposure Compensation/AEB.
2. Set the bracketing range by turning the Main dial.
3. If desired, set the exposure compensation amount by turning the Quick Control Dial 1, then press SET.
4. Take the pictures, and three bracketed shots will be created in this order: normal, underexposed, overexposed.

If you're in Single shooting drive mode, take three pictures to create the bracketed sequence. If you're in a Continuous shooting drive mode, the three shots will be taken together when you press and hold the shutter button.

Note: Bracketing will remain on until you set the bracketing range back to 0.

SLOW/FAST MOTION MOVIE

Movies can be recorded for playback in slow or fast motion. No sound is recorded.

1. Set the Mode Dial to S&F.
2. Select recording mode:

   S&F Movie Auto Exposure: Exposure is controlled automatically to suit the brightness. Record just as you would for Movie Auto Exposure.

   S&F Movie Shutter-Priority AE: Set your preferred shutter speed for slow/fast movie recording. Record just as you would for Movie Shutter-Priority AE.

   S&F Movie Aperture-Priority AE: Set your preferred aperture value for slow/fast movie recording. Record just as you would for Movie Aperture-Priority AE.

   S&F Movie Manual Exposure: Set your preferred shutter speed, aperture value, and ISO speed for slow/fast movie recording. Record just as you would for Movie Manual Exposure.
3. Select the movie recording size.
4. Select a resolution.
5. Select a recording frame rate.
6. Select a playback frame rate then press SET.

WIRELESS CONNECTION

MENU > Communication Functions (Network function) > Connect to smartphone(tablet)

Install the Camera Connect app on your smartphone and pair it with the EOS R6 Mark III. This will allow you to view and transfer images to your smartphone, see the Live View image on your smartphone, and even shoot remotely from your smartphone.

RESET CAMERA

MENU > Set-Up (Rest/All Settings) > Reset Camera

You can choose to reset individual settings or factory reset here.

1. Select movie recording format from the listed formats.
2. Select Auto Exposure to choose the shooting method:
   - **Fixed 1st Frame:** The first shot is metered, then all subsequent shots match that first shot's exposure.
   - **Each Frame:** Each frame is metered and shot separately.

05 STEP-BY-STEP SHOOTING INSTRUCTIONS

MULTIPLE EXPOSURES

Create in-camera multiple exposures:

1. Select MENU > Photo Shooting (Various Shooting) > Multiple Exposure.
2. Choose a shooting option, then press SET:

   On: Function/Control: Choose this if you want to shoot gradually and check the results as you shoot. Continuous shooting speed is lower with this option.

   On: Continuous Shooting: Choose this if you're shooting continuous multiple exposures of moving subjects.

   Disable: Choose this to turn multiple exposure mode off.
3. Choose a Multiple Exposure Control option, then press SET:

   Additive: The exposure of each image is added cumulatively.

   Average: Based on the number of exposures you set (next step), negative exposure compensation is added automatically as you shoot to achieve a standard overall exposure.

   Bright: Retains brightest portion of images.

   Dark: Retains darkest portion of images.

4. Set the number of exposures you'd like to combine, then press SET.

5. Specify whether you'd like to save all the individual images or just the resulting multiple exposure, then press SET.

6. Set a Continue Multiple Exposure option, then press SET:

   1 Shot Only: Shoot just one multiple exposure.

   Continuously: Continue shooting multiple exposures until you disable the feature.

7. Shoot all of the exposures to combine into one multiple exposure.

Note: When shooting using the Function/Control method, you can press the Preview button after taking individual shots for additional options (such as deleting the previous image so you can recapture a shot, etc.).

HDR HDR MODE

Create images with a high dynamic range with details in the highlights and shadows in high-contrast scenes. There are two HDR modes: Moving Subjects (used for photos where the subject is moving) and Dynamic Range (best for landscapes and still-life images, where the subject isn't moving). The camera takes multiple images and combines them into a single JPEG or HEIF image.

1. Select MENU > Photo Shooting (color/tone/dynamic range) > HDR Mode.

2. Choose the mode you want: Moving Subjects or Dynamic Range. When you choose Dynamic Range, you can set the following options:

   Set the Dynamic Range: The higher the number, the wider the dynamic range. Set Auto to let the camera determine the range.

   Limit Max Brightness: When turned off, the maximum brightness isn't limited and is best for viewing images on devices that have a brightness exceeding 1000 nits.

3. Select Off to stop HDR mode.

4. Take the photo: Press the shutter button all the way down and the camera will take a series of images and then automatically combine them into a single HDR image.

5. Select an option for Continuous HDR:

   1 Shot Only: You'll only shoot one HDR image.

   Every Shot: You'll continue shooting HDR images until you disable HDR shooting by selecting Off in step 2 above.

6. Select the Auto Image Align setting:

   Enable: Choose this if you're shooting handheld.

   Disable: Choose this if you're shooting on a tripod.

7. Determine if you'd like to save all the images that you shoot or just the resulting HDR image with the Save Source Images option.

TIME-LAPSE MOVIES

Create a time-lapse movie in-camera:

1. Select MENU > Movie Recording (Various shooting/Shutter control) > Time-Lapse Movie.
2. Select Time-Lapse > Enable (or Disable to turn Time-Lapse off).
3. Select Interval and enter both the shooting duration and the movie duration.
4. Set the Number of Shots you'd like to take for the time-lapse movie.
5. Select the desired Movie Recording Size (4k or Full HD).
6. Select movie recording format from the listed formats.
7. Select Auto Exposure to choose the shooting method:

   Fixed 1st Frame: The first shot is metered, then all subsequent shots match that first shot's exposure.

   Each Frame: Each frame is metered and shot separately.

8. In the Screen Auto Off option, choose Disable to have the image displayed (though the screen will automatically turn off 30 minutes after the time-lapse shooting begins); choose Enable to have the screen turn off 10 seconds after the time-lapse shooting begins.

Note: You can press the INFO button at any time during time-lapse shooting to turn the screen on and off.

9. Choose whether you'd like to hear a beep(s) after every image is captured (Beep per Image Taken). Set to 0 to turn off beeps.

10. Check your settings, then press MENU to turn off the menu screen.

11. A message will come on screen prompting you to take a test shot. Select OK.

12. Take a test shot (or two) to make sure the settings you've selected give you correct focus and exposure.

13. Press the Movie Shooting button, then press the shutter button to start shooting the time-lapse movie.

06 TYPICAL SHOOTING SCENARIOS

SHOOTING SCENARIO
PORTRAIT

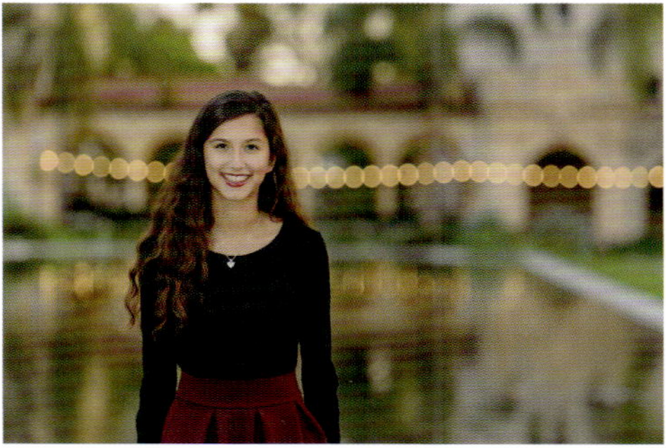

KEY PRINCIPLES

- The key to a portrait like this is shallow depth of field. Shoot in **APERTURE PRIORITY (Av)** mode and start with the lowest aperture your lens offers (such as **f/2.8 or f/4**).
- Remember to **focus on the eyes**.

- If the image is too dark or too light, use **EXPOSURE COMPENSATION** to adjust the brightness level.
- If the image is blurry from a slow shutter speed, **raise the ISO** to increase your sensor's sensitivity to light, thus allowing for a faster shutter speed.
- Remember to use a **focal length of 50mm or greater** so that you don't distort your subject's face.

SHOOTING SCENARIO
GROUP PORTRAIT

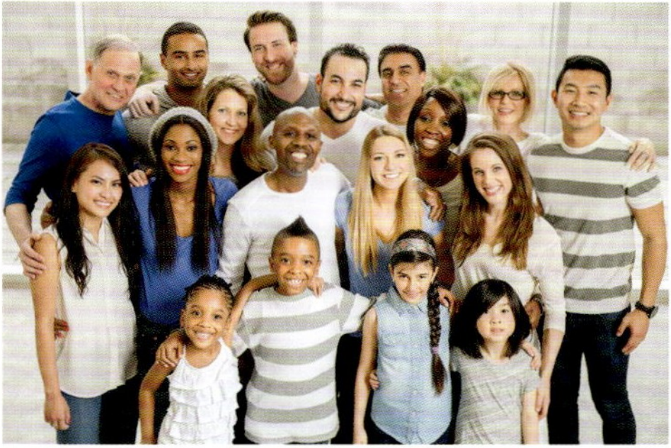

KEY PRINCIPLES

- In order to get everyone in focus, you need a deep depth of field. Shoot in **APERTURE PRIORITY (Av)** mode and set the aperture between **f/8–f/16**.
- **Focus on the person in the middle of the group**. Check the focus by using the LCD screen. View it at 100% and check faces in the front and back rows. If anyone is out of focus, use a smaller aperture for deeper depth of field.
- Use **EVALUATIVE METERING** to account for the light in the entire scene.
- **Arrange the group so they can all see you** (and you can see them).
- Use **EXPOSURE COMPENSATION** if the image is too bright or too dark.
- If the image is blurry, **raise the ISO** to allow the camera to use a faster shutter speed.

SHOOTING SCENARIO

LANDSCAPE

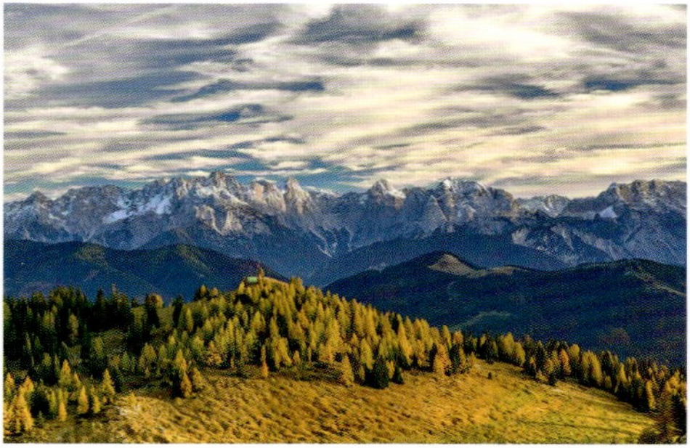

KEY PRINCIPLES

- Shoot in **APERTURE PRIORITY (Av) mode** to control depth of field. Start with **f/16** to ensure deep depth of field.
- **Use a tripod** to eliminate camera movement. Whenever your camera is on a tripod, turn **IMAGE STABILIZATION** off.
- Use **EVALUATIVE METERING** and **1-SHOT AF** focus mode.
- **Set the ISO to a low setting (100–200)** to avoid any digital noise.
- Shoot in **RAW** so that you have the most available information when editing later.
- Consider **BRACKETING** your exposures.

SHOOTING SCENARIO

FREEZE ACTION

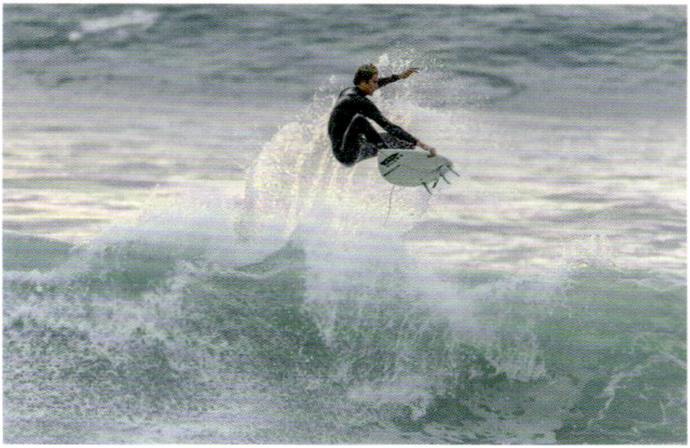

KEY PRINCIPLES

- Use **SHUTTER PRIORITY (Tv)** mode and set the shutter speed to a value that will freeze the action. The appropriate shutter speed depends on your subject and its movement, but could be anywhere between **1/500–1/8000 sec**.
- Use **SERVO** autofocus so that the camera keeps focusing as the subject moves.
- If the image is dark or blurry, **raise the ISO or try AUTO ISO** to automatically have the camera adjust the ISO as needed.

SHOOTING SCENARIO

SHOWING MOTION—PANNING

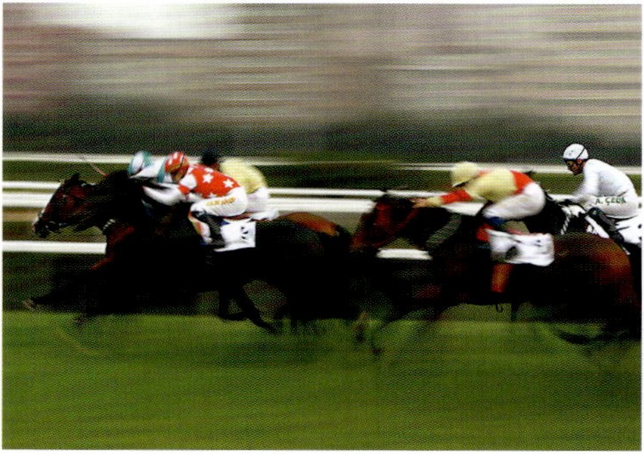

KEY PRINCIPLES

- Shoot in **SHUTTER PRIORITY (Tv)** mode and use a slow-enough shutter speed to allow for the subject to move during the exposure.
- **Follow the subject** across the frame as you shoot.
- Use **SERVO** autofocus as well as the **EXPAND AF AREA** focus mode to ensure the camera focuses on the subject. There is also a built-in panning mode as part of the Scene shooting modes.

LOW-LIGHT ACTION

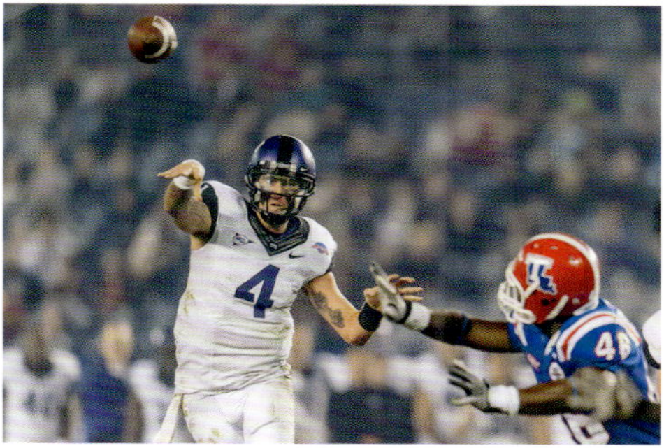

KEY PRINCIPLES

- Shoot in **APERTURE PRIORITY (Av)** mode and use a wide aperture such as **f/2.8 or f/4**.
- Use **PARTIAL METERING** and meter on the subject's face.
- Use **SERVO** autofocus and **1-POINT AF** (a single focus point).
- **Set the ISO to 1600 or higher**, depending on the amount of available light.
- If the image is blurry, **increase the ISO** to allow for a faster shutter speed.

SHOOTING SCENARIO

LONG EXPOSURE

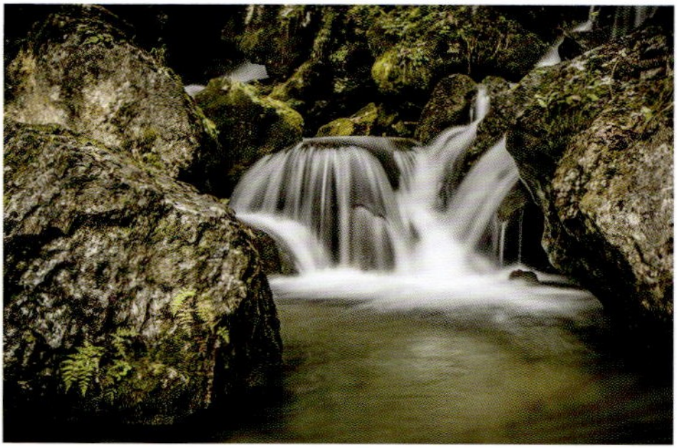

KEY PRINCIPLES

- Use **MANUAL** or **BULB** shooting mode so you can use a long shutter speed.
- **Use a tripod** to keep the camera stable and turn off any **IMAGE STABILIZATION**.
- Use the **1-SHOT AF** focus mode, or try Manual focus if the camera is having a hard time locking on focus.
- **Use a low ISO** (100–400) and **shoot RAW** to ensure a high-quality file.
- Use a **cable release** with a lock to avoid touching (shaking) the camera.

SHOOTING SCENARIO

MACRO/CLOSE-UP

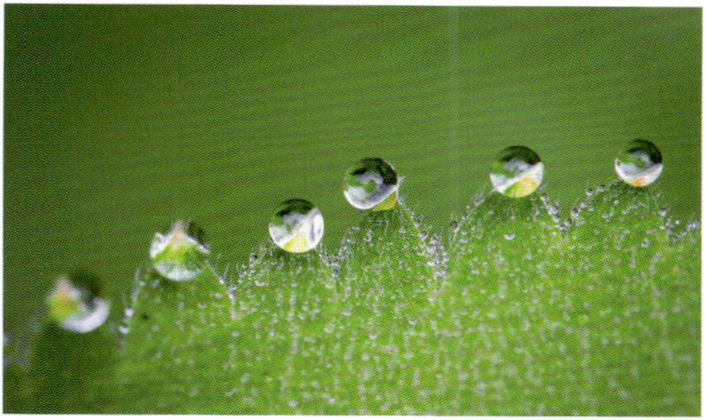

KEY PRINCIPLES

- Shoot in **APERTURE PRIORITY (Av)** mode and **use a small aperture** to ensure you achieve enough depth of field (this image was shot at f/13).
- Use **EVALUATIVE METERING** to analyze the light in the entire frame.
- A **tripod** is very useful for keeping the camera steady.
- Use **MANUAL FOCUS** and **zoom in** to confirm your focus is tack-sharp.
- Try using a dedicated **macro lens** or **close-up filters** to make sure you can achieve sharp focus when you're so close to the subject.

SHOOTING SCENARIO

VIDEO RECORDING/VLOGGING

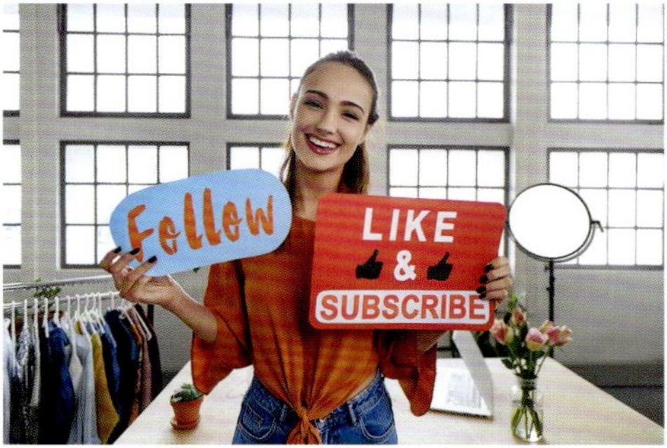

KEY PRINCIPLES

- Use a **shallow depth of field** to keep the viewers' attention on the subject. A **wide aperture** will keep the subject in focus while having the area in front of and behind the subject fall out of focus.
- Use **24 fps** for a more cinematic look.
- Set the **shutter speed to twice the frame rate** or as close as you can get. If using 24 fps, the shutter speed should be 1/50 (or 1/60) second.

- Use an **external microphone** for better sound. The Rode VideoMic GO II is a great starter microphone.
- Keep the camera stable with a **tripod or gimble**. Smooth footage looks more professional.
- Use the **swing-out monitor** to watch the video being recorded. Remember to leave 1 or 2 seconds of nothing at the beginning and end of your video clips—this will make them much easier to edit later.